FRANK LLOYD WRIGHT'S
VISION ON THE LAKE

Photo by Joe DeMaio

Madison Newspapers
INCORPORATED

Photo by L. Roger Turner

MONONA TERRACE™
FRANK LLOYD WRIGHT'S
VISION ON THE LAKE

A PICTORIAL HISTORY

Published by Madison Newspapers, Inc.
publishers of the

WISCONSIN STATE JOURNAL

and

The Capital Times

M O N O N A ■ T E R R A C E

EDITORS AND CONTRIBUTORS

Editor: **Margo O'Brien Hokanson**
Associate Editor: **Deborah Kades**
Graphic Design: **Bob Hoot,
Hoot Communications**
Photo Editor: **Meg Theno**
Introductory Essay: **Ron Seely**
Photographers:
**Joseph W. Jackson III,
Carolyn Pflasterer, Rich Rygh,
Craig Schreiner, Meg Theno,
L. Roger Turner and Joe DeMaio**
Production Coordinator:
Catherine Johnson

Special thanks: **Anthony Puttnam,
Taliesin® Architects**

On the Cover: View from Lake
Monona by **L. Roger Turner**
Thanks to Inland Boats, Inc. for their assistance
with the cover photo
Back cover photo: **Joe DeMaio**

Library of Congress Card Catalog No. 97-61051
ISBN 1-878569-43-0

Printing by Royle Communications Group, Inc.

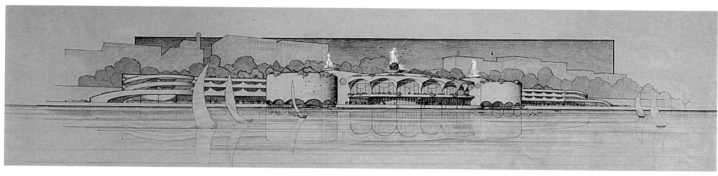

© 1997 FLW FDN

TABLE OF CONTENTS

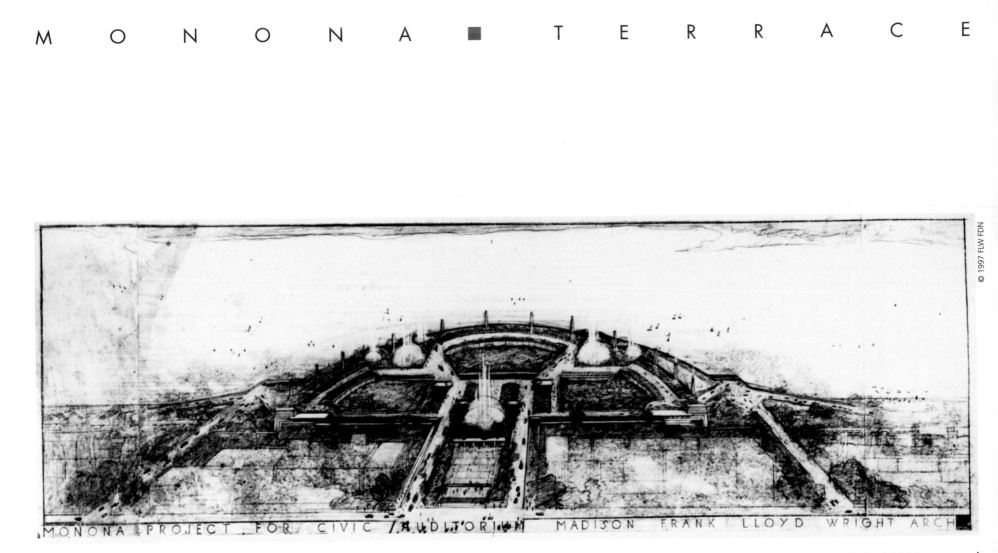

MONONA PROJECT FOR CIVIC AUDITORIUM MADISON FRANK LLOYD WRIGHT ARCH

A rendering of Frank Lloyd Wright's original 1938 proposal for a civic center on Lake Monona that he called Olin Terraces. The building was to house Madison and Dane County government offices including courtrooms and jails, and an auditorium.

THE VISION IS BORN

Rising from years of controversy, the Monona Terrace Community and Convention Center finally soars, as Frank Lloyd Wright always intended, over the blue lake. It's the work of dreamers and even now, in its white raiment of concrete, seems more dream than building.

The first dreamer, of course, was Wright himself, the cantankerous genius of an architect who broached the idea of the building at a Madison Lion's Club meeting in September 1938. The city was considering a new city-county building and Wright told the members of the civic group that he would propose "something really fine" that truly represented the "America of the future." Little did he know that the "future" would come nearly 60 years hence. This, briefly, is the story of how the dream that Wright first

Photo by John Engstead. Courtesy the Frank Lloyd Wright Archives

"Don't base this contract on the money angle. I didn't originate this plan to make money. I have none... It's all invested in an ideal..."

– Frank Lloyd Wright, 1955

spoke of in that long-ago September came to be realized.

In those days, Wright was a strange combination of pariah and prophet in Madison, the city that, more than any other in America, could lay claim to being the architect's hometown. Wright had been born in Richland Center, a farm town in southwestern Wisconsin. He had taken classes at the University of Wisconsin, briefly apprenticed with a Madison architectural firm, and then abruptly left the state for the wider world and fame. Years later, the progenitor of the distinctive Prairie School of design, Wright returned to build his home, Taliesin, on the brow of a hill overlooking the Wisconsin River near Spring Green.

Wright was frequently in nearby Madison. And he was often in the local press, mostly, it seemed, for the goings-on in his private life, which was about as unconventional as

his buildings. In the years just preceding his design of Monona Terrace, headlines tracked the fiery breakup of his second marriage and his relationship with his next wife, Olgivanna. Sweeping about town in a flowing cape and wielding a cane, Wright raised plenty of eyebrows.

Often, the architect was his own worst enemy. And so it was when he started talking about Monona Terrace. At the Lion's Club meeting, the abashed members listened as Wright — ostensibly there to convince them that they should build his building — introduced himself as "Wisconsin's black sheep" and then proceeded to denigrate Madison as "a high-browed community of provincials" whose citizens were lacking in civic spirit.

"Here," Wright proclaimed, "is a great opportunity to really build something. But that isn't what you will do.

You'll build another office building — another one of 'those things' — on a side street. Instead of putting the money into a building you'll put it into the pockets of property owners. There isn't enough civic spirit in the community to get together on something really fine, regardless of whose ox is gored and of who loses and who wins. That's the spirit that's lacking in Madison."

That was how it all started, in as odd and contentious a fashion as it would end many years later.

In contrast to Wright's harsh words, the design he worked up for the "great chance at the foot of Monona" was one of striking grace and beauty. Wright scholar Mary Jane Hamilton ranked it among the most original designs of Wright's career and "one of the more inspired urban and civic gestures of all time."

The original design was a great semi-circu-lar structure that curved out over the lake in a series of sensuous curves and terraces. It included city and county offices, courtrooms, a jail, a boathouse, and even a railroad station. Many of the features of today's convention center are recognizable from those original plans — the repeated curves and circles that echo the Capitol up the street, the domed fountains, and the lush gardens on the rooftop.

Despite the beauty and originality of the proposed building, it appeared for many years that Madison would fulfill Wright's dour prediction. Immediately after Wright's initial proposal, sides were taken and political battles begun. Delay brought about by wrangling over Wright's plan caused the loss of federal funding for the city-county building and the press was quick to pounce. Undaunted, Wright campaigned for his "dream civic center," going on the radio

"There is all the water of Lake Monona to play with, to throw up as decoration in the form of columns and fountains."

– Frank Lloyd Wright, 1941

"This scheme discovers the lake and... claims the lake for the life of the city."

– Frank Lloyd Wright, 1938

and moving a model of the structure into the State Historical Society of Wisconsin. But it was not to be; less than a year after unveiling his design, Wright put the plans away.

The same scenario was to be played out over and over in the intervening years. Wright would revive his plan numerous times — for a civic auditorium in 1941, for the city-county building (still unbuilt at the time) once again in 1948, for an auditorium and civic center in 1953.

Each time, vehement opposition led to delay and defeat of Wright's proposal. The caped architect strides through the now yellowed newspaper clippings documenting those fights. Here he is in October 1941, speaking to a group of 600 students and townspeople at the Memorial Union: "Take this venture out of politics," he encouraged the crowd. "Don't let it get into the hands of the bigshots. We must have a citizens' committee which will see that we get what we want. We need a youthful spirit."

And there he is in May 1954, talking to a group of civic leaders and "emphasizing his remarks with a borrowed cane, the head of which was a carved, bare foot."

And there he is again in November 1954, pleading with a city planning committee. At that meeting, according to the newspaper account, "Wright wore a black pinstripe suit with a high collar and a black foulard tie tucked into a brown vest. He held the floor most of the three hours of the orderly meeting. Part of the time he sat, the rest of the time he walked back and forth, now and then gesticulating with his expressive hands."

Wright had staunch supporters over the years. In 1954, supporters gathered 7,000 signatures to get the proposed building put

Frank Lloyd Wright meets with a legislative committee at the State Capitol in the mid 1950s.

Legislation pushed by Wright enemies to restrict the height of any lakeshore building to 22 feet effectively foils the project again.

Governor Gaylord Nelson repealed the legislation in 1959.

In 1938 Frank Lloyd Wright estimated the cost of building the project he called Olin Terraces at $2.75 million.

The actual construction cost of Monona Terrace was $67.1 million.

to a referendum. A University of Wisconsin professor, Edmund Zawacki, wired a loudspeaker to the top of his car and drove around the square, timing his trip to be stopped by every stoplight and reading a statement in support of Wright and his building.

But there were also motivated, crafty opponents. Two men, especially, would engage in a veritable war with Wright — Carroll Metzner, a lawyer who was also on the Madison City Council and in the state Legislature, and Joseph W. Jackson, who managed his family's Jackson Clinic in Madison.

Metzner held up the building for several years — even after the 1954 referendum was approved — by passing a bill that limited the height of any building on the isthmus side of Lake Monona to 22 feet. He was supported over the years by Jackson,

who even waged a campaign in which he tried to portray Wright as a Communist.

Wright's years-long battle to build his dream ended with his death in April 1959. It is proof of the strength of his vision, however, that others carried on after his passing. There were more failed attempts, more referendums, more political squabbles. Finally, in the fall of 1992 came the final fight. Once again forces lined up for and against a plan to build Wright's center at the foot of what was now Martin Luther King Jr. Boulevard. A group called "It Ain't Wright" formed to oppose the plan. A group called "It's Wright for Wisconsin" campaigned in favor, waging a $200,000 campaign to build the $67-million convention center. The building was approved in a huge turnout with 53 percent of the voters approving the plan and 47 percent voting against it.

The night of the vote saw wild celebration. "This has been a party 60 years in the making," said a jubilant Mayor Paul Soglin, who had been a strong proponent of the building.

But, just as the refusal of some not to give up on the building is testament to the power of Wright's architectural dream, the anger of others in the wake of the 1992 referendum is dramatic proof of the enduring anger that Wright's powerful personality stirred in others.

"The older people were solidly against it," said Gary Gates, a leader of the "It Ain't Wright" coalition. "Particularly if they knew Frank Lloyd Wright."

In spite of it all, Wright's vision is now made visible for all to share. Anthony Puttnam, the principal architect on the project for Wright's old firm, Taliesin Architects, said he has marveled at the beauty of the building as it materialized and he thought often of Wright and how, through all the years of struggle, the architect must have known that the building he was fighting for was a building for the ages.

"You can see why he was so excited, so terribly enthused about this building," Puttnam said. "This building is more powerful than any of us could ever have imagined."

– Ron Seely

In his lifetime, Frank Lloyd Wright earned $1,000 on Monona Terrace, the fee for his original 1938 commission. Wright estimated that he spent more than $150,000 developing Monona Terrace designs between 1938 and 1959.

*An evening view
of the futuristic
Monona Terrace
as Wright envisioned it
in this 1950s rendering.
This scheme included
an art gallery, theater
and exhibition hall.
John Nolen Drive ran along
the lake side of the building.*

FRANK LLOYD WRIGHT'S DREAM FOR A CITY

Through its long, serpentine history, the story of Monona Terrace is intertwined with the history of Madison. When Frank Lloyd Wright accepted $1,000 to design a "dream civic center" in 1938, he went back to the plan drawn in 1910 by the noted city planner John Nolen. Nolen had complained that Madison had turned its back on its lakes, and Wright adopted Nolen's vision of a wide avenue linking the Capitol to Lake Monona on what is now Martin Luther King Jr. Boulevard.

The original design, called Olin Terraces, included city and county offices, courtrooms and jails; a civic auditorium; a railroad station; boat docks; and parking. The design spurred both enthusiasm and criticism and was shelved and readjusted many times during the 59 years between its proposal and its construction.

The Wright who unveiled the plans in 1938 was a controversial figure in Madison, the city where he had spent much of his boyhood. Admired by some who appreciated his work and his directness, he was despised by others for his failure to pay his bills and his scandalous personal life.

World War II snuffed out the original project, but it resurfaced in the postwar years, again meeting stiff resistance. From 1953 through the late 1960s, politicians on both sides of the issue battled over Wright's plan, and even the state Supreme Court was pulled into the fray. Supporters continued the fight for the project even after its architect's death in 1959. By 1970, the project looked like it was down for the count.

"This new building will take character, and courage, and vision and intelligence, yes, and sympathy with the beautiful."

– Frank Lloyd Wright, 1938

Frank Lloyd Wright holds court with representatives of Madison's city planning committee in the mid-1950s as he details plans for a Monona Terrace designed for use as an auditorium and civic center.

MONONA TERRACE CHRONOLOGY – JOURNEY THROUGH THE DECADES

1910
John Nolen, the leading city planner in the United States, prepares a master plan for Madison that calls for a wide avenue lined with government buildings to connect the Capitol with Lake Monona and a lakeside park with a grand set of terraces stepping down to the lakeshore.

1938
A group of citizens who were unhappy with the city of Madison's plans for a civic center raise $1,000 to commission Frank Lloyd Wright to design an alternative. The Board of Supervisors turns it down, blocks the original proposal and thus loses $247,500 in federal funding.

1941
Madison voters support the idea of a civic center located on one of Madison's lakes. Wright resubmitted his design and an 18-member citizen group formed to publicize it. The attack on Pearl Harbor ended all talk of building a civic center.

1948
Both Dane County and the city of Madison agree to build a city-county building.

1952
Madison voters approve a bond issue to cover the city's $3 million in costs for the joint building. Wright dusts off his 1938 plan and resubmits it.

1954
The Madison Common Council again considers building an auditorium and civic center. In an advisory referendum, voters narrowly approve financing for the auditorium, and they approve Wright as architect. Wright begins to scale back the 1938 Monona Terrace design to meet the city's requirements. Wright's critics and supporters continue to battle. His contract is delayed.

1956
After two years of opponents' attempts to stall the project, Wright signs a contract with the city and makes major adjustments in the plans.

Wisconsin State Journal/The Capital Times file photos

*Frank Lloyd Wright
with a scale model
of his design for
Monona Terrace made
public at a recognition
dinner in the mid-1950s.
The two towers were
included as possible
additions to the center.*

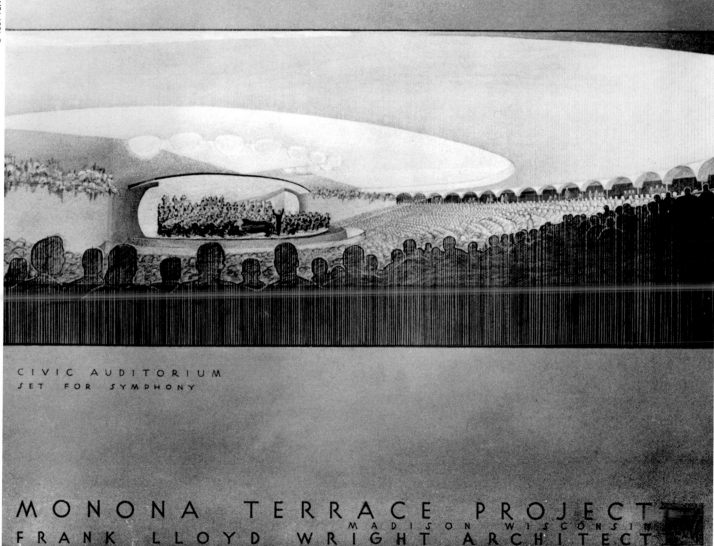

CIVIC AUDITORIUM
SET FOR SYMPHONY

MONONA TERRACE PROJECT
MADISON WISCONSIN
FRANK LLOYD WRIGHT ARCHITECT

Frank Lloyd Wright's rendering of the inside of the civic auditorium portion of Monona Terrace. This scheme was presented to the city in 1955.

Photo by Carolyn Pflasterer

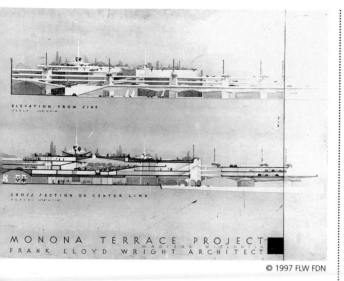

ELEVATION FROM SIDE

CROSS SECTION ON CENTER LINE

MONONA TERRACE PROJECT
FRANK LLOYD WRIGHT ARCHITECT

© 1997 FLW FDN

Left: Wright's second civic center design, featuring an auditorium and three large globe fountains symbolizing Earth, Moon and Sun, was made public in 1955 and redesigned in 1956. In later revisions, Wright added arches to the windows of the facade and the parking structure was moved back.

CHRONOLOGY

1957

Politics intrude on the project when the State Legislature passes a bill that banned construction of any lakeshore building higher than 22 feet. The state owned the lakeside parcel of land at that time.

1959

Lawsuits force the Legislature to repeal the height ban. Wright submits final design concept to city shortly before his death in April. Opponents succeed in placing the project on the ballot once again and a referendum worded so that supporters of the project must vote "no" loses soundly.

1960s

The city commissions Taliesin Associated Architects to design a 2,500-seat performing arts center. In 1961 and 1969, the auditorium section of the civic center is put up for bids but, in both cases, the bids exceed available funds. In 1969, a new mayor cancels the project.

1974

Under Mayor Paul Soglin, the city purchases two downtown buildings to be transformed into an auditorium and art center.

Photos by Joseph W. Jackson III

In the 1980s, several schemes for a convention center were proposed. Designed by different architects, all failed to pass, including this one.

In 1989 a $46 million plan to build what was then called the Nolen Terrace Convention Center was proposed. Here, former mayor Joseph Sensenbrenner discusses the plans.

CHRONOLOGY

1980s
Three attempts to build a city convention center fail. However, the Madison Civic Center on State Street opens in 1980, finally providing a civic auditorium for Madison.

1990
At the request of Mayor Soglin, Taliesin Architects analyzes the city's proposal for a convention center and determines that Wright's 1959 design for Monona Terrace is workable.

1991
Taliesin Architects is commissioned to do schematic designs for the convention center.

1992
Five decades and eight design revisions later, the Monona Terrace standoff is finally broken by Mayor Paul Soglin, who appoints a development commission with a broad cross-section of members from chief executives of utility companies and labor leaders to art students and university professors. Governor Tommy Thompson offers $18 million in state funds to pay for the parking portion of the project.

1994
Construction on Monona Terrace begins in December after Wright apprentice Anthony Puttnam of Taliesin Architects finalizes designs.

1997
Monona Terrace opens to the public in July.

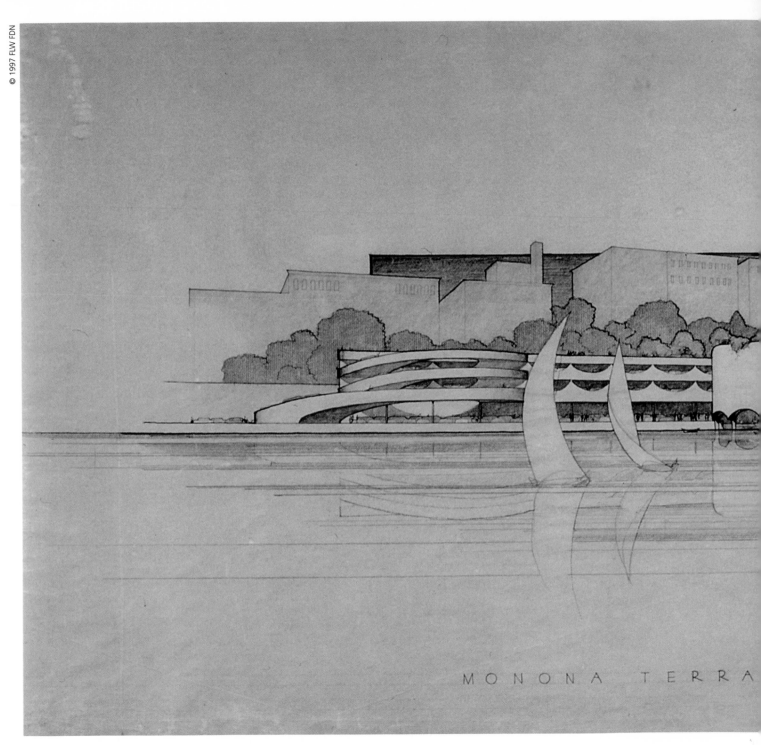

MONONA TERRA

Frank Lloyd Wright signed off on this version of Monona Terrace just weeks before his death in 1959. It was the version on which bids for the project were based in the 1960s. The rendering closely approximates the exterior of the finished building, and the basic footprint of the building did not change significantly after this time.

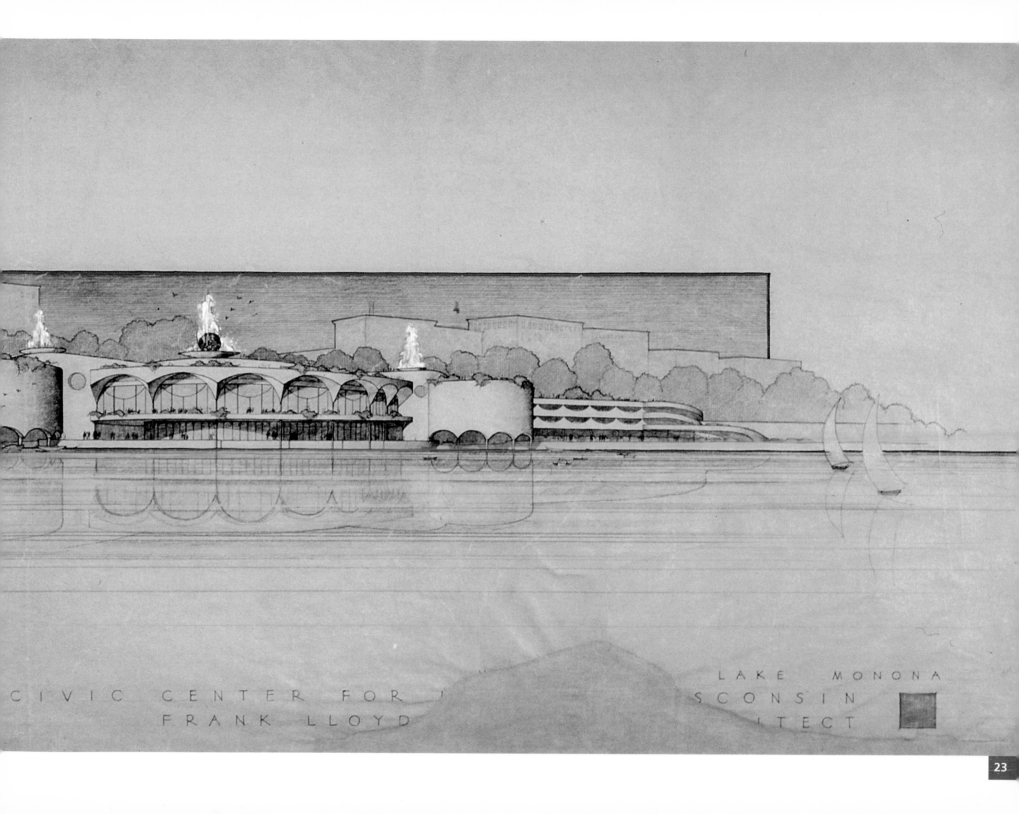

CIVIC CENTER FOR LAKE MONONA
FRANK LLOYD SCONSIN
 ITECT

23

Photo by Joseph W. Jackson III

Mayor Paul Soglin outlines his plan for the center in 1990, while contractor Orville "Bud" Arnold looks on.
This drawing by Taliesin Architects shows the convention center. At the time, estimated construction costs were $48 million.

FRANK LLOYD WRIGHT'S DREAM BECOMES A MADISON REALITY

When the convention center project was revived in the 1990s by Madison Mayor Paul Soglin, the climate of the city had changed. Soglin, in office for the second time after taking a hiatus from politics, was perhaps older and wiser, and so was the city itself.

But not everything had changed. Madison remained as divided a city as ever. Only this time, the more conservative faction favored the Wright-designed project. Business people felt that a convention center designed by the world's most famous architect would prove to be a valuable draw, bringing people and revenue into Madison. Monona Terrace lost the support of many liberals, who feared the project might pose a threat to the environment, and who were concerned about the overall cost of such a project relative to other community needs.

What was different in the 1990s was the city's ability to move forward. With the mayor, the county executive, the governor and the private sector behind it, the project was approved by voters in a 1992 referendum and ground was broken in December 1994.

Anthony Puttnam, the project's design principal, says that Frank Lloyd Wright would want Madisonians to look at the convention center as a beginning not an end, that he would want the city to look for more opportunities for exciting architecture.

Wright himself had no illusions about the obstacles his "dream civic center" faced, nor did he doubt that his plan was right for the city. "They'll never build Monona Terrace in my lifetime," he would say, adding, "But, someday they will."

"Blessings could flow to the city, the state and to the whole country from this development, for no other city has anything like the chance Madison has to take advantage of the lakes."

— Frank Lloyd Wright

Photo by Joseph W. Jackson III

Anthony Puttnam, one-time Frank Lloyd Wright apprentice and design principal of Monona Terrace, with an illustration of the design for the building.

RECALLING THE VISION:
ANTHONY PUTTNAM BRINGS PROJECT TO LIFE

The Monona Terrace project challenges people's ideas about Frank Lloyd Wright, says Anthony Puttnam, a member of Taliesin Architects and the design principal for the project.

"Usually we think of Mr. Wright going to the country to escape the city," explains Puttnam, pointing out Wright's close ties to Spring Green. "Here, in Monona Terrace, he is reinforcing the fabric of the city."

There is probably no person better suited to speak of the famed architect than Puttnam, who came to Taliesin in 1953 and worked on the Monona Terrace drawings and models for a few years before heading to New York City. He came back after Wright's death to help with drawings for the 1961 bid and ended up staying.

Puttnam clearly has not lost sight of his mentor's vision. "Mr. Wright set out to make Monona Terrace resonate architecturally with the State Capitol. All the design elements echo the Capitol, like the domes and the arches."

Recalling the days when he worked with Wright at Taliesin, Puttnam smiles. "Anyone who was around the project came away with the feeling that it was fun, that Mr. Wright was enjoying it. He had a wry appreciation of the fact that it probably wouldn't get built."

But don't ask Puttnam to speak for Wright. Asked what Wright would say if he saw the project as it has been executed, Puttnam replied tersely, "You'll have to ask him."

And it is no accident that Puttnam always puts a Mr. in front of Wright. "Someone pointed out that the entire architectural world does that," Puttnam says. "Only people who didn't respect him said 'Wright.'"

"It's a courageous building. And in the context of Madison it is a very courageous building."

— Anthony Puttnam, one-time Frank Lloyd Wright apprentice and design principal of Monona Terrace

Monona Terrace Community and Convention Center was created by Monona Terrace Design Venture, an association of Taliesin Architects, Potter Lawson Architects, and Arnold and O'Sheridan, Inc., Consulting Engineers.

Photo by L. Roger Turner

A model of Monona Terrace, unveiled in June 1992 to coincide with the 125th anniversary of Wright's birth, launched a campaign to win voter approval to finance part of the cost of the center.

Photo by L. Roger Turner

JUNE 1992

This kiosk in the State Capitol displayed architectural renderings of the proposed convention center and was part of the campaign to convince area voters to pass the funding referendum.

SEPTEMBER 1994

Site preparation had already begun prior to the official groundbreaking.

Photo by Joseph W. Jackson III

OCTOBER 1994

Far right: Mayor Paul Soglin presides over the "groundbreaking" ceremony. The event was purposely low-key due to the continued controversy over the project.

Photo by Joseph W. Jackson III

Photo by Meg Theno

Photo by Joseph W. Jackson III

JANUARY 1995

*Law Park stretched out uninterrupted along the west side of Lake Monona
as machinery began to gather to start construction of Monona Terrace.*

MAY 1995

*Lake lovers had the perfect vantage point from which to watch
the convention center rise along the shore of Lake Monona.*

Photo by Carolyn Pflasterer

Photo by Carolyn Pflasterer

MAY 1995

*Left: Pilings had to be driven into the ground
to form support for the framework of the project.
In the meantime, opponents were mounting
another unsuccessful electoral bid to stop construction.*

*Above and right: Thousands of hours of labor
and hundreds of hands were required to do
the seemingly endless tasks required to
bring Frank Lloyd Wright's dream to life.*

MAY 1995

An employee of Ed Kraemer and Sons used an electronic distance measuring device to survey for placement of pilings.

35

JUNE 1995
*With exacting care,
workers make sure
steel support beams
are solidly in place.*

MAY 1995
*The underpinnings of
Monona Terrace began
to take shape in late spring 1995
as steel and concrete support
columns were erected at the east
side of the building.*

Photo by Joseph W. Jackson III

Photo by Joseph W. Jackson III

JUNE 1995

Beams rose high above Lake Monona as men and machines positioned the building's framework.

Photo by Joseph W. Jackson III

JUNE 1995

As the glistening framework of Monona Terrace rose,
Madisonians could see how the convention center would harmonize with the lake.

JUNE 1995

The building's curves, designed to reflect the State Capitol building, swell outward over the waters of Lake Monona as architectural details emerge from the steel support beams.

Photos by Joseph W. Jackson III

Photo by Joseph W. Jackson III

Photo by Joseph W. Jackson III

SEPTEMBER 1995
By early fall, J.H. Findorff & Sons was building the overall structural framing and preparing to enclose the building.

JUNE 1995
Workers prepare to pour the final overlayment of concrete.

OCTOBER 1995
As the framing rose, the drama of Wright's design was poised to emerge.

DECEMBER 1995

A demure Christmas tree hinted at the celebrations to come at Monona Terrace.

JANUARY 1996

J.H. Findorff & Sons workers carefully lowered the first of eight concrete bowls, each 8 feet in diameter, into place on the rooftop garden railing. The 68,000 square foot plaza is accessible to the public at street level.

Photo by Joseph W. Jackson III

JANUARY 1996

As Madison moved into 1996, the convention center began to take shape with the erection of concrete arches and the placement of light bowls.

Photo by Joseph W. Jackson III

MARCH 1996

Monona Terrace affords a new view
of the State Capitol and downtown Madison.

Photo by Carolyn Pflasterer

MAY 1996

By spring 1996, windows on the lake side of the building provided breathtaking vistas of Lake Monona. "It's just a beautiful place," commented one of the Dane County supervisors who toured the work in progress in May 1996.

Photo by Joseph W. Jackson III

Photo by Craig Schreiner

JUNE 1996

Final touches are put on one of two 34-foot light dishes that adorn the top of Monona Terrace. Part of the original design from the 1930s, the dishes are covered with plastic domes and reflect light from other rooftop sources.

AUGUST 1996

With a perfect view of the construction, two fishermen started the weekend early on a warm Friday afternoon.

Photo by Joseph W. Jackson III

JUNE 1996
*Wide curves characterize the walkways
that bring visitors into Monona Terrace.*

Photo by Joseph W. Jackson III

AUGUST 1996
By late summer 1996, an aerial view of the Isthmus revealed how gracefully Monona Terrace unites with the shore of Lake Monona.

SEPTEMBER 1996
Right: A Findorff worker aligns tiles in Madison's version of Hollywood's sidewalk of stars. About 8,000 personalized tiles had been purchased by the time the convention center opened in July 1997.

Photo by Joseph W. Jackson III

CLAIMING A PIECE OF HISTORY

When Mary Lang-Sollinger visited Seattle in 1991, a friend took her downtown to see a tile with a personal message that had been laid as part of a floor in Pike's Place market.

"We couldn't find the tile, but we spent the better part of the day there, visiting landmarks, shopping, having lunch," said Lang-Sollinger.

A State Street property owner, Lang-Sollinger has long been active in Downtown Madison so it's no surprise that her thoughts turned to home. "On the plane back to Madison, I thought, this would be great for Madison. People would bring visitors to Monona Terrace to see their tile."

A core group of about 20 came together to form the Friends of Monona Terrace. Selling tiles in two sizes, the volunteers and a few paid staffers sold 8,000 tiles in two campaigns in 1995 and 1996.

The cement tiles in one- and two-square-foot sizes can be found on the rooftop garden and the pedestrian bridge. They feature names, dates and messages such as "Happy Birthday" and "Go Badgers."

Proceeds from the tile sales helped pay for amenities and finishings for the convention center, including an upgraded chandelier in the ballroom, more and more mature plantings for the rooftop garden and decorative waste containers.

The price of the tiles was kept as low as $50 to allow as many people as possible to participate. "The price was part of giving people a sense of belonging," Lang-Sollinger says.

People from 33 states and seven countries, including Germany and Puerto Rico, purchased tiles after hearing about the project over the Internet and through the national press.

Says Lang-Sollinger, "It was amazing."

Photo by Joseph W. Jackson III

JANUARY 1997
*In early 1997, lunchtime hockey players could enjoy
the sweeping panorama of Monona Terrace while they played.*

NOVEMBER 1996
*All the major components of Monona Terrace
were visible by the end of 1996.*

MAY 1997
Visitors to Monona Terrace enjoy the whimsical maze-like design of the rooftop.

APRIL 1997
Frank Lloyd Wright deliberately designed the arches on Monona Terrace to echo the curving lines on the state's Capitol.

Photo by Joseph W. Jackson III

Photo by L. Roger Turner

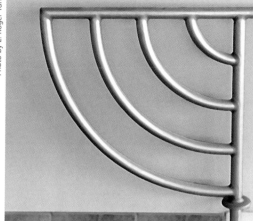

*Detail of inside
stairway railing.*

MAY 1997

*Newly elected Dane County Executive Kathleen Falk
and others, led by Rich Lynch of J.H. Findorff & Sons,
tour Monona Terrace as it nears completion.*

Photo by Joe DeMaio

The entry helix to the parking ramp is evocative of the Guggenheim Museum in New York City. Monona Terrace was first designed in the 1930s, contemporary with Wright's work on the Guggenheim.

Photo by L. Roger Turner

Thirty-four-foot-tall arched windows provide a spectacular view of Lake Monona.

Right: Sweeping curves with intricate geometric detailing are the signature feature of the Lecture Hall on Level Four, which seats 320 people.

Photo by L. Roger Turner

Photos by L. Roger Turner

*Custom-designed
carpeting, echoing
the wave pattern found
on design elements
throughout the building,
guides the way through
the Capitol Promenade
to the Grand Terrace.*

Photos courtesy of Taliesin® Architects

Above: A nighttime view of Monona Terrace's rooftop, aglow in futuristic splendor.

Right: The majestic facade of Monona Terrace, summer 1997.

Photo by L. Roger Turner

Detail from the ceiling of the most expansive room inside the convention center, the Exhibition Hall. The room can accommodate more than 4,000 people for receptions.

Photo by Joe DeMaio

Monona Terrace's rooftop garden features 8,000 engraved tiles free-floated over a special waterproof surface to protect them from the freeze/thaw cycle.

Monona Terrace extends 90 feet from the shoreline of Lake Monona, fanning out over approximately six acres of water.

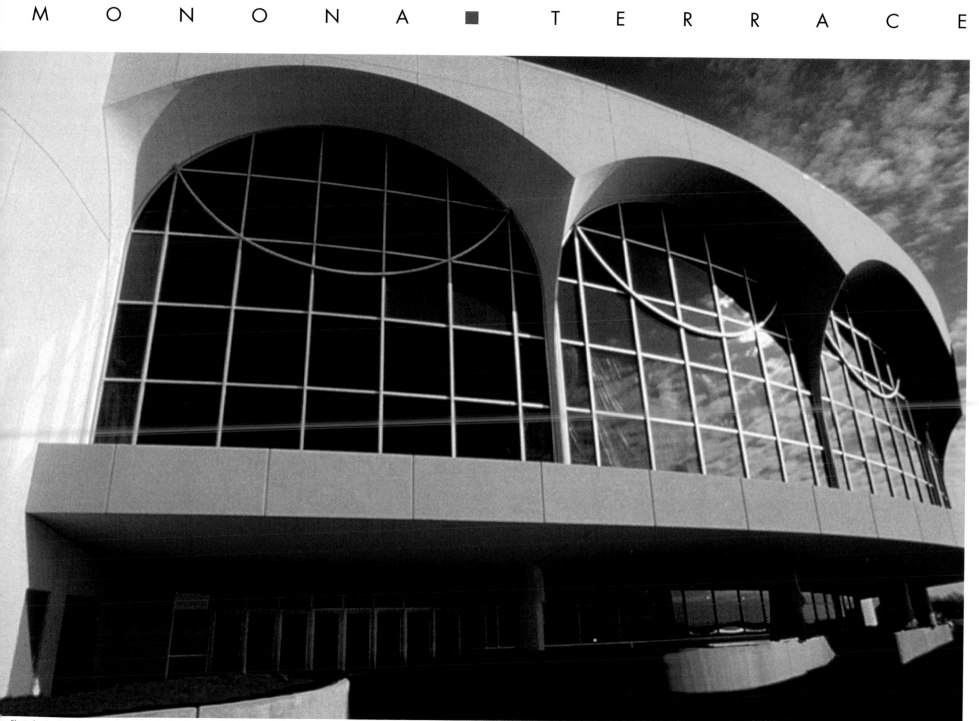

Photo by Joe DeMaio

UNITARIAN MEETING HOUSE
900 UNIVERSITY BAY DRIVE
MADISON
1947

*The American Institute of Architects
considers this one of the most
significant buildings that Wright designed.
Wright insisted on locating it
in Shorewood Hills, then a suburb
three miles west of downtown Madison,
so he could design a building that
complemented its surroundings.
Society members provided sweat equity
and Wright gave benefit lectures
to underwrite the building,
which exceeded the original estimate
by almost 400 percent.*

FRANK LLOYD WRIGHT: MADISON WORKS

Internationally acclaimed architect Frank Lloyd Wright designed more than 1,100 works, including houses, office buildings, churches, schools, libraries, museums and bridges. His extant buildings in Madison include the Unitarian Meeting House, Herbert Jacobs House I, Herbert Jacobs House II, Eugene Gilmore House, John Pew House and the Robert Lamp House.

More than one-third of his buildings in the United States are listed on the National Register of Historic Places or are in a National Historic District. Fourteen of his buildings are National Historic Landmarks.

EUGENE GILMORE HOUSE
120 ELY PLACE
MADISON
1908

The classic Prairie School home was built when Wright's Oak Park career was at its zenith. Known to locals as "the airplane house" it went up on a lot in the new subdivision of University Heights that boasted spectacular views of three lakes, the Capitol, and the University of Wisconsin.

Photos by Rich Rygh

THE HERBERT JACOBS
HOUSE 1
441 TOEPFER AVENUE
MADISON
1936

This modest house in Madison's Westmorland neighborhood demonstrates Wright's interest in building affordable homes. Built for a Madison newspaper reporter, the 1,300-square-foot design uses the grid system that Wright would find increasingly attractive.

THE JOHN PEW HOUSE
3650 LAKE MENDOTA
DRIVE
SHOREWOOD HILLS
1939

The John Pew House is only 1,300 square feet but its dramatic position makes it look larger. Architectural historians have admired the house, which hugs the ground at one end of a sloping lot and extends over a ravine at the other, seemingly hanging in mid-air.

W R I G H T   I N   M A D I S O N

THE HERBERT JACOBS
HOUSE II
3995 SHAWN TRAIL
MIDDLETON
1944

In the shape of a half circle, this home offers breathtaking views of the blanket of farmland surrounding the lot. An earth berm protects the northern, outside expanse, while the southern wall boasts large windows and glass doors. A circular pool is half inside and half outside the house.

FRANK LLOYD WRIGHT'S VISION ON THE LAKE

For additional copies of this book
and for other titles on Madison and Dane County,
call or write Madison Newspapers Promotions Department:
(608) 252-6249
P.O. Box 8056, Madison, WI 53708